OUTDOOR PLANTS

RP MINIS

PHILADELPHIA

RP Minis®
Hachette Book Group
1290 Avenue of the Americas, New York, NY 10104
www.runningpress.com
@Running_Press

First edition: April 2023

Published by RP Minis, an imprint of Perseus Books, LLC, a
subsidiary of Hachette Book Group, Inc. The RP Minis name
and logo is a registered trademark of the Hachette Book Group.

The Hachette Speakers Bureau provides a wide range
of authors for speaking events. To find out more, go to
www.hachettespeakersbureau.com or call (866) 376-6591.

The publisher is not responsible for websites (or their content)
that are not owned by the publisher.

ISBN: 978-0-7624-8228-3

CONTENTS

Introduction:
The Joy of Outdoor Plants . . . 7

Power Plants: Fascinating Facts
about Outdoor Plants . . . 11

100 Incredible Outdoor Plants . . . 16

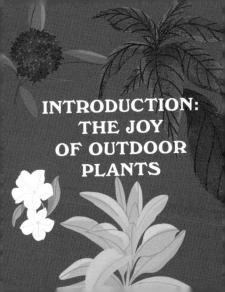

INTRODUCTION:
THE JOY
OF OUTDOOR
PLANTS

> ## "Where flowers bloom,
> ## so does hope."
> **—LADY BIRD JOHNSON**

Welcome to the wonderful world of outdoor plants! Creating a green scene outdoors isn't just about aesthetics— plants can clean the air, attract pollinators, repel pests, and could increase your property value! From fabulous foliage plants to cute and compact container specimens to fast-growing backyard dominators, there's a plant for every personality.

In this mini book, you'll learn some fascinating facts about outdoor plants and read all about 100 amazing varieties, ranging from some of the most popular standards to unusual specimens that are truly not your garden variety.

Each entry in this book gives you the opportunity to learn about a different outdoor plant. You'll learn how it looks, some of its notable traits, and, in some cases, a few care tips. For more detailed information on tending to plants, please refer to *Plant Care*. Ready to turn over a new leaf? Here we go!

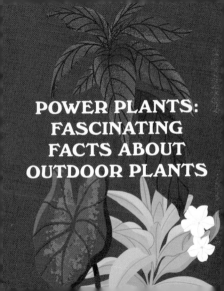

POWER PLANTS: FASCINATING FACTS ABOUT OUTDOOR PLANTS

1. Plants can talk to each other.

Plants may not be able to talk, but they can definitely communicate with one another. For instance, say a plant is experiencing an aphid infestation. It can exude small amounts of chemicals that will effectively raise the alarm bell for the surrounding root zone, allowing its plant neighbors to take defensive measures to ward off the attack.

2. Plants create market crashes.

Ever heard of tulip mania? When tulips were first introduced to Holland in the 1600s, people went bonkers for these bulbs. At a certain point, some varieties were more valuable than gold! A system of ever-mounting prices that led to buying on credit was not sustainable, and the market eventually crashed. Today, tulips are far more affordable.

3. Plants don't need us as much as we need them.

Plants aren't just ornamental! The majority of the earth's oxygen comes from plants, both above and below the ocean's surface. Without them, we wouldn't have air to breathe. On the flip side, they'd mostly fare just fine without us.

4. Most plants live underwater.

Did you know that roughly 85 percent of the earth's plant life lives in the ocean? It makes sense when you consider that much of the planet is covered by water. But it's mind-boggling to consider that the wide array of outdoor plants is a mere fraction of the plant life out there.

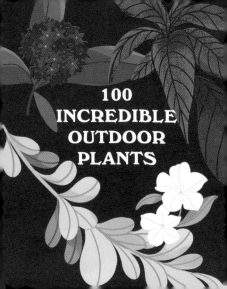

100 INCREDIBLE OUTDOOR PLANTS

1/ ASTER
Symphyotrichum

It's easy to get all starry-eyed about this flowering plant, which takes its common name from the ancient Greek word for *star*, referring to its dainty little daisy-like flower heads, which often feature white, blue, and purple petals. Though it's often sold as a seasonal fall flower, it can be a long-lived perennial if well cared for.

2/ AZALEA
Rhododendron

This shrub brightens shady spots with vibrant, funnel-shaped flowers that come in a variety of tones scattered throughout thick, dark green foliage. This hardy plant will bloom year after year in the right conditions. Fun fact: It used to be considered a death threat to send someone azalea or its close relative, rhododendron, owing to their toxicity.

3/ BALLOON FLOWER
Platycodon grandiflorus

Before blooming, this plant's buds
look like a colony of tiny hot-air
balloons. Eventually, they unfurl
into blue-violet, star-shaped flowers
that last all summer long. This
clump-forming perennial plant
is ideal for beginning gardeners.
Typically planted in the spring, it
blooms quickly and will reward you
with beautiful flowers even in the
first year.

4/ BEE BALM
Monarda didyma

This perennial, a relative of the mint plant, has brightly colored flowers with tubular petals that look like mini fireworks. Both flowers and stems are highly aromatic, which makes them a magnet for bees, butterflies, and hummingbirds. They're also used in herbal medicine and culinary applications. This plant grows quickly, but be warned that in some areas it is considered invasive.

5/ BEGONIA
Begonia semperflorens

Sometimes referred to as "wax begonia," owing to its waxy green, bronze, or maroon leaves, this bush-like plant has fluffy clusters of flowers that are usually pink or white. It's desirable as a low-maintenance outdoor plant that is deer-resistant and doesn't require much pruning. In warm and humid climates, it can be a perennial; otherwise, it's grown as an annual.

6/ BLUE SPRUCE STONECROP
Sedum reflexum

If you love the ease and look of succulents but don't live in a hot climate, stonecrops are the perfect pick. This low-growing variety has a bluish-green color, spruce-like needles, and a spreading tendency. It grows extremely well in stony, rocky settings. It prefers a sunny spot, but it's winter-hardy and can withstand frigid temperatures.

7/ BOSTON IVY
Parthenocissus tricuspidata

This plant puts the *ivy* in *Ivy League*—literally—and is the stuff you'll see covering venerable institutions of higher learning. It's a climbing vine that will cling to just about anything and will tolerate just about any conditions—warm, cold, sun, shade. In some areas, it's considered a lovely climber or ground cover; in other regions, it's viewed as invasive.

8/ BOUGAINVILLEA
Bougainvillea

What look like papery-textured
flowers in vibrant tones of pink,
purple, and orange are actually
petal-like bracts that hide the
bougainvillea's actual blooms—
unassuming and tiny white or yellow
flowers. This sprawling shrub prefers
conditions that mimic its native
tropical habitat. In cooler climates,
it can be grown in containers and
moved indoors in the winter.

9/ BOXWOOD
Buxus

Adorable isn't often a word used to describe shrubs, but boxwood fits the bill. It's a choice pick for shaping into topiaries. While it comes in countless varieties, it's generally famed for its compact green leaves and rounded, densely packed growth that gives it an overall fuzzy texture. It can survive winters in cooler climates, though it may thin out.

10/ BUTTERFLY WEED
Asclepias tuberosa

This glossy-leaved perennial plant is a butterfly magnet! It blooms in the spring and summer with puffs of bright orange and yellow star-shaped flowers that are rich in nectar and pollen. Despite the name, it's not fast-growing—the *weed* means it's a type of milkweed. It can tolerate cold winters but can take a few years to become established.

11/ CALADIUM
Caladium

The fabulous foliage of caladium
has no equal, with huge yet delicate
arrow-shaped leaves that come
in a stunning array of colors and
patterns from paint-spattered to
striped or deeply veined varieties.
It's a perennial in warmer climates,
but in cooler climates it can be
brought indoors, or you can dig up
its tubers and replant in the spring.

12/ CALENDULA
Calendula officinalis

This plant is a relative of the daisy, as evidenced by its flowers with delicate petals and serrated-looking edges, usually in yellow or orange. It can be a short-lived perennial in warm climates, but it's usually grown as a rapidly flowering annual. Not just a looker, calendula is edible and also has medicinal properties; it is used in topical ointments to treat skin conditions.

13/ CAMELLIA
Camellia

This slow-growing shrub that thrives in partial shade features dark, glossy leaves and generously petaled blooms resembling a mix of peonies and roses, that come in a variety of different colors. Believe it or not, camellia's been around for thousands of years, and each plant can live for over a century. This plant prefers moderate temperatures, though some varieties are cold-hardy.

14/ CANNA LILY
Canna

Despite its showy, tubular, and decidedly lily-like flowers, this sun-loving plant isn't technically a lily. Further, despite its flowers, its foliage is the real draw—massive variegated leaves that take on a stained-glass appearance when the sun shines through. It can be a perennial or an annual in warmer climates, or it can be brought indoors in cooler climates.

15/ CATMINT
Nepeta

Considered a cat aphrodisiac, this aromatic perennial herb has a delicate appearance, with lacy-looking foliage and spikes of white, pink, or blue-green that bloom in the early summer. However, despite its delicate appearance, it's an extremely sturdy and cold-hardy plant that's easy to grow; it is also deer-resistant. With a tendency to sprawl, it's a popular plant for edging areas.

16/ CENTURY PLANT
Agave americana

This supersized succulent has
a distinct midcentury-modern
aesthetic, with large, blue-green
leaves emerging in a rosette pattern
that look like tentacles with tiny
spines on the ends. While slow-
growing, this plant's life span is
more like 30 years than an actual
century. While it will tolerate
drought-like conditions, it won't
tolerate frost or high humidity.

17/ CIGAR PLANT
Cuphea ignea

With bright-red flowers with black tips, this plant's flowers somewhat resemble glowing cigars, extending from dense branches with delicate leaves. It's a choice plant for attracting butterflies, hummingbirds, and other pollinators and is a perennial that will flower year-round in a tropical climate. Elsewhere, it can be grown in containers and moved inside for the winter or treated like an annual.

18/ CLEMATIS
Clematis

Clematis is best-known as a climbing plant—in fact, the name comes from an ancient Greek term that roughly translates as "vine" or "branch." The most classic version features big flowers with intricate centers and pointy-ended, somewhat papery petals atop a bed of bright-green, arrow-shaped leaves. Temperature tolerance depends on the variety.

19/ COCKSCOMB
Celosia

With its unique, plumage-like shape and velvety, bright blooms, it's not hard to see why this plant is named after a rooster's tail (comb). The blooms can be red, yellow, pink, or white, and the alternating, arrow-like leaves are often green but sometimes bronze-toned. While it's frequently grown as an annual in cooler climates, cockscomb can be perennial in warmer climates.

20/ COLEUS
Coleus scutellarioides

This plant is a window-box classic, with fabulous foliage, featuring unusual, striking, multicolor patterns that can range from graphic to quilt-like. While it can produce tiny blue or white flowers, they're sometimes pinched off so they don't distract from the famed foliage. This fast-growing plant is considered an annual in cooler climates, though it can be a perennial in warmer climates.

21/ COLUMBINE
Aquilegia

This plant's singular blooms have rounded inner petals and an outer layer of pointed petals that resemble jaunty caps resting atop foliage that resembles clovers. They're known and prized for their ability to attract hummingbirds. They have a fairly short growing season, but if you avoid deadheading them, they could self-sow and create a whole new generation.

22/ CONEFLOWER
Echinacea purpurea

This plant's daisy-like blooms have purplish-pink petals that turn downward from the flower head, sometimes giving them a shape like a badminton shuttlecock. While this perennial will grow and sprout leaves quickly, it probably won't flower for a few years. However, once they do bloom, the season is long and they're extremely hardy. All parts of this plant are edible.

23/ CORAL BELLS
Heuchera

This perennial plant, with distinctive, somewhat doily-shaped leaves that have etched-looking veins, takes its name from the bell-shaped flowers that grow on its long, upright stems, usually in a deep-coral color. Native to North America, this versatile plant works equally well as a ground cover or a border and is a magnet for butterflies and hummingbirds.

24/ CREEPING JENNY
Lysimachia nummularia

This creeping perennial plant features bright-chartreuse leaves that resemble little coins. While it can grow tiny yellow flowers, it's best known for its foliage and its hardiness—it's able to tolerate both heat and cold. It's easy to grow and hard to kill, and works well as a hanging plant, as a container plant, or as a ground cover.

25/ CROCUS

Crocus

Considered a harbinger of spring, this low-growing perennial bulb is one of the season's earliest bloomers. Resembling tiny tulips, these delicate flowers come in many colors, including lavender, pink, yellow, and white. They're also easy to grow—when planted in the early fall, they can bloom in two to five weeks after the temperature rises in the early spring.

26/ DAFFODIL
Narcissus

Even before spring's in full swing, you'll see daffodils. This seasonal icon's flowers feature a trumpet-shaped center within a radiant sunburst of petals in any combination of white, yellow, or orange. These easy-to-care-for perennial bulbs can be planted in the fall and will put on a sunny show the following year, peaking shortly after the final frost.

27/ DAHLIA
Dahlia

Dahlias have edible tubers—in fact, they were originally classified as a vegetable! These late-season bloomers have big, showy, and intricate petal displays that almost look kaleidoscopic. They come in a variety of colors and shapes, and some flowers are as big as a salad plate. They're a perennial in warm climates but are often treated as an annual.

28/ DAYLILY
Hemerocallis

Despite their distinctly lily-like appearance, daylilies are not considered "true" lilies. The name refers to their look and their short life span—the flowers open in the morning and wither at night. A prolific perennial, the daylily comes in most colors of the rainbow, is extremely easy to grow, is tolerant of both under- and overwatering, and can take extreme heat.

29/ DWARF ALBERTA SPRUCE
Picea glauca 'Conica'

Need a little Christmas, right this very minute? The dwarf Alberta spruce is an adorable Christmas tree–shaped plant with a distinctive, earthy aroma and a densely packed growth habit that gives it a wooly appearance. Though it can eventually reach upward of 10 feet, it grows very slowly and can be kept in a large container for years.

30/ EASTERN PRICKLY PEAR CACTUS
Opuntia humifusa

This classic-looking cactus has large, green, paddle-like segments patterned with wedge-like spikes and produces lovely rose-like flowers in the summertime. Like many cacti, it's drought-resistant and loves a lot of bright light. Despite its sunny southwestern look, it can tolerate below-freezing temperatures.

31/ EDELWEISS
Leontopodium alpinum

This perennial plant has delicate flowers that look like little twinkling stars against a backdrop of fuzzy-textured, lance-shaped leaves. But don't let appearances fool you—these flowers are far tougher than they look. They thrive in harsh climates like the northern Alps and are fully capable of withstanding high wind, frigid temperatures, and rocky soil.

32/ FAIRY DUSTER
Calliandra eriophylla

If fairies had little pink feather
dusters to clean their homes, they'd
probably resemble the whimsical-
looking blooms that dot the
fern-like foliage on this shrub each
spring. Despite its fanciful and
feathery appearance, this desert
native is actually quite hardy—it
has a dense root structure and can
withstand drought conditions,
gravelly soil, and bright sun.

33/ FALSE INDIGO
Baptisia australis

It's not indigo, but this wildflower provides a passable and less costly substitute for its dye; hence, the name. It has proud, upright stems with gray-green leaves and clusters of violet-colored, sweetpea-like blossoms. After blooming, black seed pods remain that can be left on for aesthetic appeal in the winter.

34/ FAN FLOWER
Scaevola aemula

This shrub's leaves almost look like flowers themselves, with clusters of lance-shaped leaves arranged rosette-style. But there's no missing the actual blooms, which have a semicircle of petals that look like a series of extended, old-fashioned hand fans. This warm-weather perennial or annual performs remarkably in the summer and can easily continue to bloom in temperatures over 100°F.

31.

33.

37.

41.

38.

32.

40.

35.

34.

39.

36.

35/ FIDDLEHEAD FERN
Matteuccia struthiopteris

Not only does it look incredible, but it's also edible! Each stem of this bright-green fern unfurls from a tightly coiled "fiddlehead"—as they're commonly called, thanks to their resemblance to the scroll of a violin or fiddle—into a unique, upright growth habit. It grows quickly; while it's a perennial, the edible season only lasts a few weeks.

36/ FORSYTHIA
Forsythia

The flowers come before the leaves on this low-maintenance shrub, giving you an unobstructed view of its impressive display of many tiny yellow, star-shaped blooms. As they fade, you get a continued show of small pointed leaves through the fall. Forsythia is a fast grower, gaining as much as 2 feet per year and a total height of 10 feet.

37/ FOUR O'CLOCKS
Mirabilis jalapa

This plant is almost like a morning glory in reverse—its bright, trumpet-shaped flowers typically open in the afternoon and party all night before closing up in the morning. They come in a variety of colors, including multicolored varieties. This warm-weather perennial or annual grows quickly and often sprawls in the garden, though it doesn't climb like the morning glory.

38/ FOXGLOVE
Digitalis purpurea

This plant has tall stems, featuring a multitude of bell-shaped flowers, often in purple, with tiny spots on the inside. As for the name, some say it's inspired by the person who classified it; others claim it refers to its flower size, which is ideal for fox accessories. It's typically considered a biennial. Beware, however: All parts of this plant are toxic.

39/ FOXTAIL FERN
Asparagus densiflorus

Lush, fluffy stems, growing upright, give this plant the look of a collection of foxtails in fern form. Technically, it's part of the asparagus family and not a thirsty fern at all, which explains why it can withstand drought conditions. It can be a perennial in a warm, humid climate; elsewhere, it needs to be brought inside for the winter.

40/ FRINGE FLOWER
Loropetalum chinense

This evergreen shrub takes its
name from its colorful flowers
that have unusual fringed petals.
In the spring, the blooms overtake
the foliage and give the plant a
fluffy, ethereal look; for the rest of
the year, the bright-green foliage
provides visual interest. This
plant prefers partial shade and can
withstand moderate cold in
the winters.

41/ FUCHSIA
Fuchsia

Strung along slender, leafy stems, fuchsia flowers look like tiny, flamboyant fairy homes—neon pink sepals that unfurl to reveal a second layer of purple petals and elegantly drooping stamens. Not only does this warm-weather perennial or cool-weather annual provide a welcome pop of color in the fall, but it thrives in shady conditions that would challenge other plants.

42/ GARDEN CHRYSANTHEMUM

Chrysanthemum

In the fall, vibrant and richly colored chrysanthemum displays abound in garden centers. The blooms resemble tight, compact daisies, understandable since they are part of the same family. While mums are often treated as an annual and left to die off in the winter, they're actually a hardy perennial that can be planted in the spring and begin blooming in the fall.

43/ GARDEN PINKS
Dianthus plumarius

This plant's flowers aren't always pink, so what's with the name? Some say the name comes from the flowers' fringed edges, which look like they were cut with pinking shears. While its blooming season is short-lived, it's an easy plant—the fast-growing perennial can emerge in under two weeks and could be in bloom a month or so after.

44/ GARDENIA
Gardenia jasminoides

This flowering shrub is famed for its fragile, highly fragranced white flowers that somewhat resemble roses and provide a stunning visual against the plant's glossy green foliage. It doesn't tolerate cold very well, so if you're in a cool climate, bring it indoors for the winter. Take note: Gardenia plants don't tolerate transplanting very well, so be careful when you're repotting.

45/ GHOST PLANT
Graptopetalum paraguayense

When you get close, you'll see that
the leaves of this rosette-shaped
succulent have an unusual powdery
texture—that ghostly glow is
what gives this plant its name. In
its native Mexico, it's long been
considered an ornamental outdoor
evergreen; in cooler climates, it can
live in a container outdoors during
the summer and come inside for
the winter.

46/ GLOBE THISTLE
Echinops

The spiky, blue-gray orb-like blooms of the globe thistle somewhat resemble medieval spike balls atop tall stems with prickly leaves. But don't be scared off—this plant is actually quite welcoming to pollinators like bees and butterflies while effectively deterring deer. It's a relatively low-maintenance perennial that can handle many soil types and withstand brutal winter conditions.

42.

46.

50.

45.

44.

47.

48.

49.

43.

47/ GOLD DUST PLANT
Aucuba japonica

This shrub, native to Japan, is extremely photogenic, with thick, glossy, dark-green, elongated leaves with irregular speckles of golden yellow. It's also extremely slow-growing; it may take years to mature and reach full size. Patience is necessary, but hard work isn't—this plant is extremely hardy, thrives in cool and shady locations, and doesn't require much care.

48/ GOLDEN BAMBOO
Phyllostachys aurea

Sometimes referred to as "fairyland bamboo," this fast-growing perennial plant has woody, golden stems topped with an abundance of lance-shaped leaves. It can grow up to 20 feet tall, allowing you to create a secret garden right in your backyard. It can be difficult to curtail its growth in warm and humid areas, but cooler climates can keep it under control.

49/ HEAVENLY BAMBOO
Nandina domestica

With cane-like stems and delicate leaves, it certainly looks like bamboo, but it's not. This ethereally named ornamental evergreen shrub can provide four seasons of visual intrigue—white flowers in spring, red berries in the winter, and leaves that change color as the seasons change. It can survive a frost, but in colder climates, move it indoors for the winter.

50/ HELIOTROPE
Heliotropium

Clusters of tiny, delicate, starburst-shaped purple or white flowers grow in the direction of the sun's rays, which explains their name. In Greek, *helios* means "sun," and *tropos* means "to turn." The scent is just as intoxicating as the flowers, giving it another nickname—"cherry pie plant." This warm-weather perennial is often grown as an annual in cooler climates.

51/ HOLLYHOCK
Alcea rosea

Hollyhock is in the same family as hibiscus—the resemblance is evident in its showy blooms in bright colors with dazzling centers. However, unlike hibiscus, hollyhock grows on very tall stems (some up to eight feet high!) and can handle some low temperatures. While it's a biennial, it is able to self-seed, meaning it will provide seeds to regrow every year.

52/ HOPS
Humulus lupulus

This visually pleasing and sun-loving perennial vine will grow vigorously on a trellis and features large, deeply veined green leaves as well as the tiny cones that are so highly prized in beer making (be sure to get a female plant if that's your goal). More than just a brewing ingredient, its edible shoots both resemble and can be cooked like asparagus.

53/ HOSTA

Hosta

This plant is likable without being too showy, composed of a lush bunch of elongated, green, heart-shaped leaves, often with white streaks. It may produce lily-like blooms, but the foliage is the main attraction. It's an extremely popular perennial, thanks to its easygoing nature; it grows quickly, can tolerate cold, is easy to propagate, and thrives in shady spots.

54/ HYACINTH

Hyacinthus orientalis

This perennial bulb plant is not shy.
While its intensely bright, tubular,
starburst-shaped flowers in white,
pink, or purple, and long, slender,
bright-green leaves are eye-catching,
the scent commands just as much
attention. For some, the heavy,
highly aromatic scent of this early-
season bloomer is a welcome sign of
spring—for others, the scent is a bit
overwhelming.

55/ HYDRANGEA
Hydrangea

Madonna may not be a fan—
she once stated that she loathes
hydrangeas—but there's a lot to love
about this big and beautiful shrub,
featuring large pom-pom–shaped
flower clusters that might be blue,
chartreuse, pink, purple, or white,
sometimes with multiple colors on
the same plant. Hydrangea is a rapid
grower that requires minimal care
and can withstand low temperatures.

56/ ICE PLANT
Delosperma

Despite its name, the ice plant doesn't shy away from the sun. When light reflects off the tiny hairs on its fleshy, succulent-style foliage, it can resemble frosty ice crystals. In sunny areas, the ice plant will issue bright, daisy-like blooms from spring through summer. The fast-growing ice plant has a tendency to spread, making it a great ground cover.

57/ IMPATIENS
Impatiens

These spring and early-summer bloomers have abundant foliage, punctuated by a number of flowers with clover leaf–like petals that come in several bright colors and in two-toned varieties. Its prolific blooming habit, ability to thrive in the shade, and minimal care requirements make impatiens very popular in annual gardens and window boxes, though it can be a perennial in warmer areas.

58/ IRIS

Iris

This flowering plant's iconic blooms feature upward-facing petals, called "standards," paired with downward-facing petals, called "falls." The most classic color is bluish purple, but they actually come in a wide array of shapes and colors; the genus includes over 300 varieties. Most irises prefer full sun and generous watering but can tolerate a variety of different temperature zones.

59/ LAMB'S EAR
Stachys byzantina

This perennial plant gets its name from the texture of its silvery-green foliage, which is soft and fuzzy. When several are planted together, it lends a soft texture and mat-like appearance to your garden; since it spreads quickly, it's often used as a ground cover or border. It loves the sun and can tolerate a number of temperature zones.

60/ LANTANA
Lantana camara

Clusters of tiny day-glo flowers make up the distinctive hemisphere-shaped blooms on this butterfly magnet of a plant. Sometimes they're a single color; other times, a spectacular mix. The branches and leaves are similarly distinctive—the sprawling appearance of the woody branches is vine-like, making them a popular hanging-basket option. This warm-weather perennial is treated as an annual in some climates.

61/ LAVENDER
Lavandula

With its gray-green foliage and upright flower spikes, featuring delicate purple blooms, this herbaceous perennial looks as good as it smells and is often used in herbal remedies and in culinary applications. While lavender's life span is usually less than 10 years, it's an easy-to-grow perennial that can tolerate many weather fluctuations and acts as a deer repellent.

62/ LILAC

Syringa vulgaris

The light-purple color lilac takes its name from this plant, famous for its aromatic branching clusters of tiny flowers, which can also be white or pink, and bright-green, heart-shaped leaves. This woody-branched shrub can tolerate winter cold; if pruned and given adequate sun, it can grow up to 12 feet high.

63/ LILY OF THE VALLEY
Convallaria majalis

Fairy flower alert! This plant boasts delicate flowers that branch off umbrella handle–shaped stems and look like little white bells. Despite the name, it's not a true lily; in fact, it's more closely related to asparagus (though it's not edible). Tougher than it looks, lily of the valley is a hardy perennial that spreads quickly and will keep coming back even in colder climates.

64/ LOBELIA
Lobelia erinus

The delicate petals of this plant's tiny flowers have a distinct orchid-like vibe and come in a variety of colors, including blue, pink, purple, and white, often with an accent color in the center. Not only is this trailing perennial prized for its ability to bloom in both full sun or partial shade, but it's also used as an herbal remedy.

65/ LUPINE
Lupinus

There's no ignoring these showy springtime wildflowers, with unusual towering cone-shaped clusters of blooms that come in a variety of colors and lovely foliage that is reminiscent of palm leaves. This fast-growing and sun-loving flowering plant, which is part of the pea family, can be an annual or perennial in warm climates and will attract bees, butterflies, and hummingbirds.

66/ MAHONIA
Berberis aquifolium

It's four seasons of fun with this shade-loving evergreen shrub. In the spring, you'll see clusters of fuzzy yellow flowers. In the summer, it yields highly tart but edible purple-blue fruit, which gives the plant the nickname Oregon grape. Green and burgundy foliage provides visual delight for the rest of the year. This plant attracts bees, butterflies, and hummingbirds.

66.

64.

62.

65.

67.

70.

69.

63.

61.

68.

67/ MEADOWSWEET
Spirea

It's not hard to see why this woody perennial shrub is often grown ornamentally: Its countless lilliputian flower clusters with delicate centers create an overall fuzzy appearance emerging from bright-green leaves. It's also a magnet for fluttering pollinators, though it's not deer-resistant. It's long been considered medicinal and is used to treat stomach acid and other stomach issues.

68/ MORNING GLORY
Ipomoea purpurea

This clinging, flowering vine has trumpet-shaped flowers that come in a variety of colors or are sometimes multicolored. At night, the buds are tightly wound, like a closed umbrella, but they unfurl in the morning when the sun hits them, giving them their name. There aren't many easier plants out there—these annuals grow prolifically and self-sow, and butterflies and hummingbirds love them.

69/ MOSS ROSE
Portulaca grandiflora

Don't be fooled by the name—
this plant isn't a rose at all but
a flowering succulent. It has
abundant foliage, featuring
rounded green leaves, which can
spread to create a dense mat or
ground cover. In the summer, it
has bright, multicolored flowers
with ruffled petals that resemble
tiny roses. This succulent is both
heat- and drought-resistant.

70/ NASTURTIUM
Tropaeolum

This plant's cheerful, bold-colored flowers somewhat resemble mini hibiscus and are like pops of color poking out from oodles of rounded green leaves. But they don't just look good, they're edible, too, with a peppery taste that can be used in salads and other culinary applications. This annual is very easy to grow and thrives on a certain level of neglect.

71/ ORNAMENTAL KALE
Brassica oleracea

Technically, ornamental kale is edible, but take one bite and you'll see that it was bred for looks, not flavor. It may taste bitter, but the visual is sweet—rosettes of green, purple, rose, and cream tones that blur the line between vegetable and flower. This cool weather–friendly annual or biennial is a popular fall or winter addition to window boxes or gardens.

72/ ORNAMENTAL PEPPER
Capsicum annuum

This spicy plant cuts a pleasing profile, with skinny green leaves and peppers that range from finger-shaped to plump and rounded that come in a variety of colors, including red, yellow, and purple. But despite the "ornamental" label, these peppers are, in fact, edible. This sun-loving plant is a perennial in warm climates but is often treated as an annual.

73/ PANSY
Viola × wittrockiana

These brightly colored flowers look delicate, with soft, overlapping, heart-shaped petals with inner markings, but they're actually quite sturdy. They can withstand less-than-ideal soil conditions and are fairly cold-tolerant, which makes them a popular springtime plant, though too much heat and humidity may make them wilt. This plant can be perennial but is often treated as an annual.

74/ PAPYRUS
Cyperus papyrus

Papyrus is often thought of as an ornamental grass, with its long, tall, triangular stems with branching-off stalks that resemble fireworks on top. But it's technically a sedge, or a cousin of grass. It may produce subtle flowers in the summer, but it's mostly a foliage plant. Papyrus does best in warm, wet, and boggy conditions.

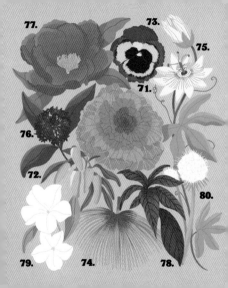

75/ PASSION FLOWER
Passiflora

If you're looking for a plant with wow appeal, look no further than this vigorous, vining perennial. Its namesake blooms are truly spectacular, with a wide, flat flower head encircled by flat petals topped with an inner ring of dainty, string-like petals. These singular sensations usually remain open for only a day unless in the right conditions.

76/ PENTAS
Pentas lanceolata

It's not hard to see why this perennial plant is also called "Egyptian star cluster"; it has shallow and distinctively star-shaped blooms that grow in clusters and come in a variety of colors. Its unusual anatomy lets pollinators easily dip into many flowers quickly for maximum nectar access. Part of the same family as coffee, this perennial won't tolerate extreme cold.

77/ PEONY
Paeonia

Starting as tight little balls, peonies slowly unfurl into large, showy blooms with layer upon layer of fluffy petals and an intoxicating scent. This low-maintenance perennial grows slowly but can live for up to 100 years. Fun fact: It's said that this plant came to be when the Greek god Zeus rescued a student from a jealous teacher's wrath by turning him into a peony.

78/ PERSIAN SHIELD

Strobilanthes dyerianus

This plant's rich, purplish-green leaves with distinctive veins are shaped like tiny shields of armor, poised for battle; an iridescent sheen heightens the effect. Tiny blue flowers may bloom, but the foliage is the real star attraction. In hot climates, it's evergreen; in cooler climates, it can be brought indoors for the winter.

79/ PETUNIA

Petunia

With wide, trumpet-shaped flowers that come in a vast array of shapes and color variations and branching foliage, this wildly popular and prolific annual makes a pretty addition to beds, borders, and containers from spring through fall. Gross fact: Petunia is related to tobacco! In fact, the word *petunia* is derived from a native South American term for "tobacco."

80/ RATTLESNAKE MASTER

Eryngium yuccifolium

Looking for an unusual plant that will add intrigue to your garden without too much maintenance? Rattlesnake master it is. In the summer, its orb-shaped flower heads bloom with many tiny flowers. This plant may initially look like a thistle, but it's actually related to carrots. It's a low-maintenance perennial that can tolerate a variety of temperature zones.

81/ ROSE
Rosa

Roses are red ... and pink, purple,
yellow, and just about every color
in between, and they come in a vast
array of different forms, including
shrubs, miniature plants, and
even climbing varieties. They're as
famous for their scent as they are
for their blooms. Regardless of type,
roses usually need a lot of sun and
frequent watering, though well-
draining soil is key.

82/ ROSEMARY

Salvia rosmarinus

This shrub's distinctive grayish-blue-green leaves may resemble evergreen needles, but they have a soft texture. An evergreen in its native Mediterranean setting, it prefers warm and relatively humid conditions. In very cold climates, it should be brought indoors for the winter. This plant's aromatic leaves are common in medicinal and culinary applications.

83/ SAGE
Salvia officinalis

With velvet-textured, grayish-green, aromatic leaves and densely packed flower spikes with blue-purple blooms in the summer, this semi-shrubby perennial plant is as attractive as it is easy to grow. Provided it's in a sunny and relatively dry spot, it won't need much active care. Its leaves are widely used in both herbal remedies and culinary applications.

84/ SEA THRIFT
Armeria maritima

This perennial plant takes its name from its natural habitat—it comes from the coastal cliffs of northern Europe. While its grass-like foliage is fetching, it really shines during the summer months when it blooms with bright and perky, sphere-like flower clusters in pink, purple, red, or white. Its care is undemanding, and it can tolerate some salt in the soil.

85/ SENSITIVE PLANT
Mimosa pudica

Few plants would be described
as shy, but this warm-weather
perennial with fern-like foliage
and purple flowers that resemble
pom-poms definitely fits the bill.
The tiny hairs on top of the leaves
are extremely sensitive to things
like touch and will visibly shrink by
folding inward when touched. In
cool climates, it's an annual or
a houseplant.

86/ SHASTA DAISY
Leucanthemum × superbum

While, technically, this is a hybrid, it's just about the most classic-looking daisy you can find, with tender white petals around a cheerful, sunny yellow center. This plant is easy to grow, can tolerate partial shade, and pollinators love it. While it's hardy and can withstand harsh winters, this plant is a short-lived perennial that will need to be replanted every few years.

87/ SHOWY LADY'S SLIPPER

Cypripedium reginae

Interested in growing orchids but don't live in a warm, humid climate? This is the plant for you. These flowers, which resemble dainty shoes that a princess might wear to a ball, can withstand brutal winters; in fact, it's the official state flower of Minnesota. Native to mossy woodland conditions, this hardy perennial prefers dappled sunlight.

88/ SNAIL VINE
Cochliasanthus caracalla

This eye-catching, vining plant features distinctive flowers that spiral out from a snail-shell shape into beautiful, abstract-looking blooms in white, lavender, and cream colors. It's a fast grower that tends to cling, so it needs a support structure, such as a trellis, and it has to be kept in check lest it take over your garden. Snail vine will not tolerate frost.

89/ SNAPDRAGON
Antirrhinum majus

If you pinch one of this plant's brightly colored and unusually shaped flowers, it will open like the mouth of a mythical beast; hence, the name. Its singular blooms grow on stems that can reach up to four feet high and feature lance-like green leaves. Though it can be a perennial in warmer climates, it's often grown as an annual.

90/ SPUR FLOWER
Plectranthus

This shrub-like plant has thick, sturdy stems featuring distinctive leaves that are gray-green on the top and purple on the bottom and intense bluish-purple flowers that bloom from spur-like buds. These versatile and low-maintenance plants will thrive in a variety of conditions and can grow several feet high but must be treated as an annual or brought inside in cooler climates.

91/ SUNFLOWER
Helianthus

Did you know that sunflowers actually angle their flower faces toward the sun? These summery flowers have large, disk-like flower heads composed of many tiny blooms that are ringed by sunny-hued petals sitting atop thick stems with rough-textured leaves. No surprise: Sunflowers love full sun and can tolerate dryness. Once they decline, their seeds provide bird food all fall long.

92/ SWEET POTATO VINE
Ipomoea batatas

While this fast-growing vine is part of the same species as sweet potatoes, it's usually planted for visual appeal rather than its edible tubers. While many varieties exist, perhaps one of the most recognizable forms features heart-shaped leaves in an eye-popping chartreuse hue. With its bright tendrils that pour over the sides of containers, it's a favorite for window boxes.

93/ TI PLANT
Cordyline fruticosa

According to legend, the more stalks on your ti plant, the more good fortune you'll have in life. Luckily, this plant grows quickly and features spectacularly colored green and hot-pink leaves that may extend more than a foot long. Take note that this is a warm-weather evergreen; if the temperature dips below 50°F, bring it inside.

94/ TICKSEED
Coreopsis

This summer annual or warm-weather perennial grows in clumps that include several stems of cheerful flowers that resemble daisies. The most classic version is a buttery-yellow flower with ruffle-edged petals. As for its connection to ticks? The plant takes its name from its round seeds that somewhat resemble them, though it's more likely to actually attract bees and birds.

94.

100.

91.

96.

99.

95.

98.

93.

92.

97.

95/ TULIP
Tulipa

These perennial flowering bulbs are the stuff of legend: Drinking glasses are named after their signature bloom shape, and they were once considered more valuable than gold! Tulips are planted in the fall and bloom in the spring to reveal their classic, cup-shaped flowers on slender buds, surrounded by strap-like leaves. There are thousands of colors and types available.

96/ WISHBONE FLOWER
Torenia fournieri

This annual plant is a wish come true if you're looking to brighten up a shady spot in your garden. It takes its name from its pretty, trumpet-shaped flowers' distinctive double stamen, which resembles a wishbone. The flowers, which come in a variety of colors, will bloom during the summer months, provided they receive adequate water, but otherwise require little maintenance.

97/ WISTERIA
Wisteria frutescens

This romantic and enchanting vine features cascading clusters of sweet-scented, blue-purple blooms and shiny green leaves that are often seen growing on pergolas or archways. Unlike Chinese wisteria, which is sometimes considered invasive, American wisteria is a lot less aggressive. While it's fast-growing and can ultimately reach 30 feet in length, it may take years to flower.

98/ YARROW
Achillea millefolium

This sun-loving, herbaceous, perennial plant has serious southwest vibes, with its feathery, fern-like leaves and tall stalks with clusters of tiny flowers that come in a variety of colors and bloom in late spring or early summer. Some find its pungent scent pleasant and chrysanthemum-like, while others say it stinks. It's referred to as "nature's neosporin" for its medicinal properties.

99/ YEW
Taxus baccata

Perhaps the most classic version of this plant is English yew, which has a distinctly holly-jolly look, with bright evergreen needles, cones, and tiny red berries. It's an easy-to-grow-and-care-for shrub, but be forewarned: It's ornamental only. Yew is infamous for its toxicity; in fact, in the Harry Potter series, yew was the wood used in Voldemort's wand!

100/ ZINNIA
Zinnia elegans

Loud and proud is the name of the game for these annuals, which come in a variety of eye-popping colors and intricately layered petal formations. Related to the sunflower, they grow on a much smaller scale, but share similar, rough-textured leaves. Zinnias grow quickly, require little maintenance, and can withstand poor growing conditions, making them a late-summer favorite.

This book has been bound using handcraft methods and Smyth-sewn to ensure durability.

Written by
Jessie Oleson Moore.

Illustrated by Lucila Perini.

Rosemary image
page 109 © iStock / Getty Images
Plus / Arif_Vector

Designed by
Amanda Richmond.